The design contains the following mirrored text (readable in a mirror):

- LOVE
- A QUILT FROM ALL OF US
- TO
- ♡ MADE WITH LOVE BY ♡
- IN THE YEAR OF:
- IN THE CITY AND STATE OF:

Note: Design message can be read more easily by holding it up to a mirror.

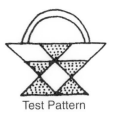

Test Pattern

A QUILT FROM ALL OF US

May your sorrows be patched
and your joys quilted ♥

Patched and quilted by

In the year

QUILT NAME

PIECED BY

QUILTED BY

DATE:
LOCATION:

3

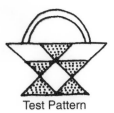

Test Pattern

Quilted from
the heart and hand
of

In the year

In the state of

A Remembrance

Quilted with love by:

In the year:

When this you see
remember me

Appliqued
with love by

Test Pattern

15

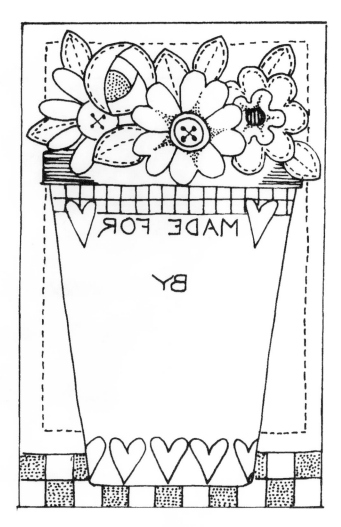

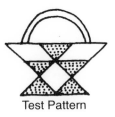

Test Pattern

One who sleeps under a quilt...

is comforted by love

THIS QUILT MADE ESPECIALLY FOR

MADE WITH LOVE BY

IN THE YEAR

AT

MADE ESPECIALLY FOR

MADE BY YOUR LOVING GRANDMA

DATE:

LOVE

A token of Affection
for
Made by

Life is a quilt sewn
together with memories

A true friend is forever a friend

Test Pattern

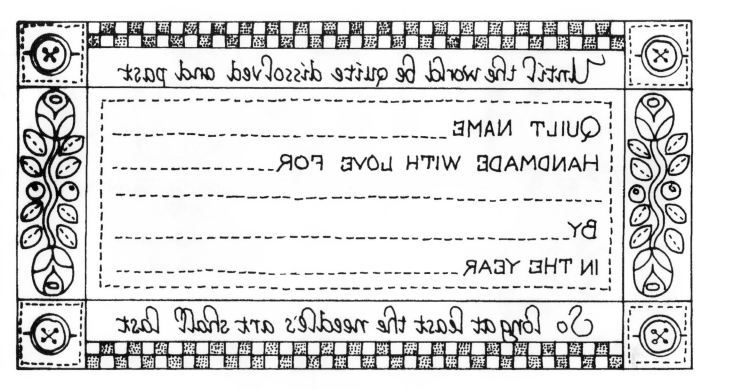

Until the world be quite dissolved and past

QUILT NAME _____
HANDMADE WITH LOVE FOR _____
_____
BY _____
IN THE YEAR _____

So long at least the needles art shall last

A QUILT JUST FOR YOU

MADE WITH LOVE BY _____

IN _____

Test Pattern

25

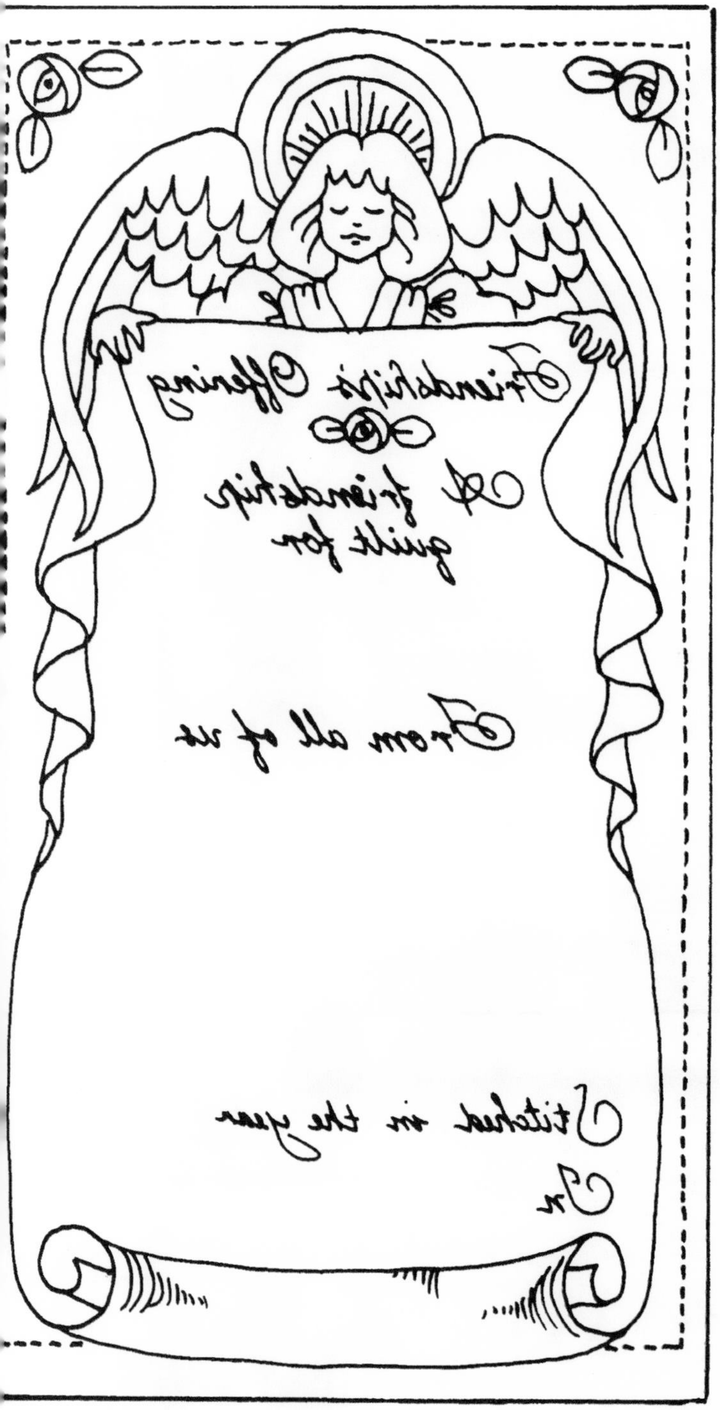

Friendship Offering

A Friendship
quilt for

From all of us

Stitched in the year

In

Made with love by

In

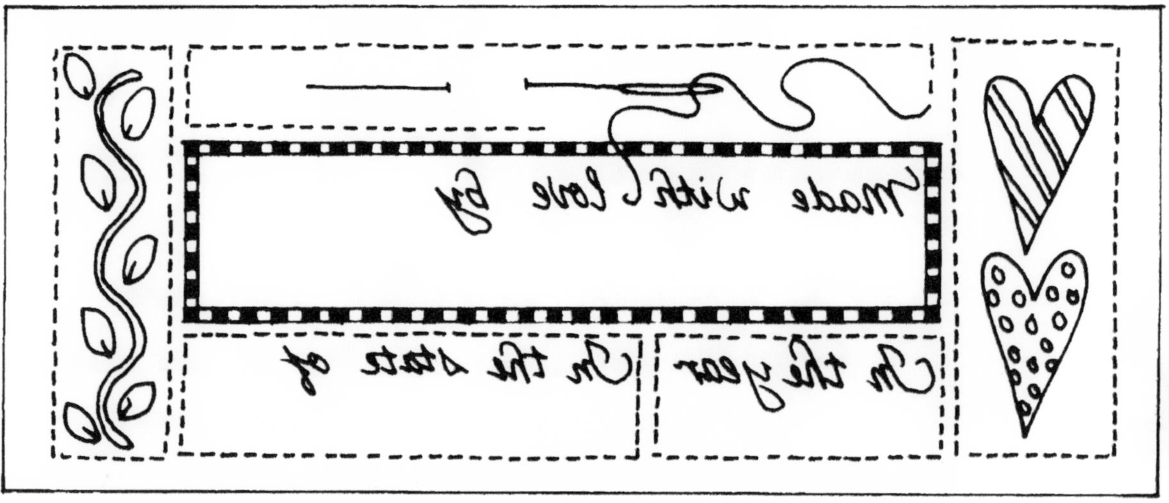

Made with love by

In the year   In the state of

Home, the spot of earth supremely blest,
A dearer, sweeter spot than all the rest.

QUILT NAME

MADE FOR:
MADE BY:
YEAR:
CITY & STATE:

The memories we collect and give
Brighten our lives as long as we live.
Julie Sneyd

Test Pattern

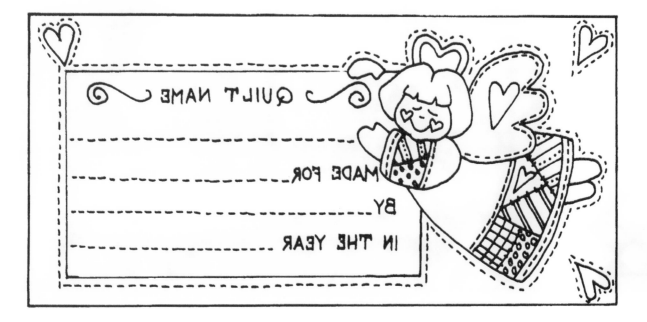

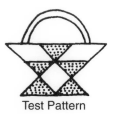

Test Pattern

THERE'S A DESTINY THAT MAKES US BROTHERS
NONE GOES HIS WAY ALONE
ALL THAT WE SEND INTO THE LIVES OF OTHERS
WILL COME BACK INTO OUR OWN.
Edwin Markham

To

From all of us

date

A quilt is a blanket of love

Test Pattern

QUILTS AND FRIENDS ARE LIFETIME TREASURES

MADE WITH LOVE
BY

A mini from the
hand and heart of:

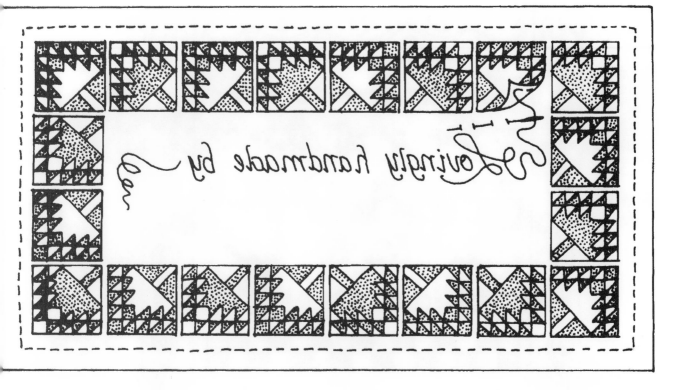

Lovingly handmade by

Wash by itself in mild soap
It was ever a quilt thing
flops — Hang to dry through
Young for ABC 1971

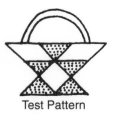

Test Pattern

What comes from the heart
Goes to the heart ♥

From the heart and hand of

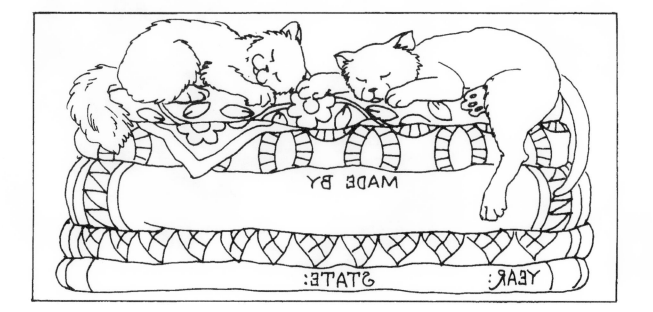

MADE BY

YEAR: STATE:

41

43

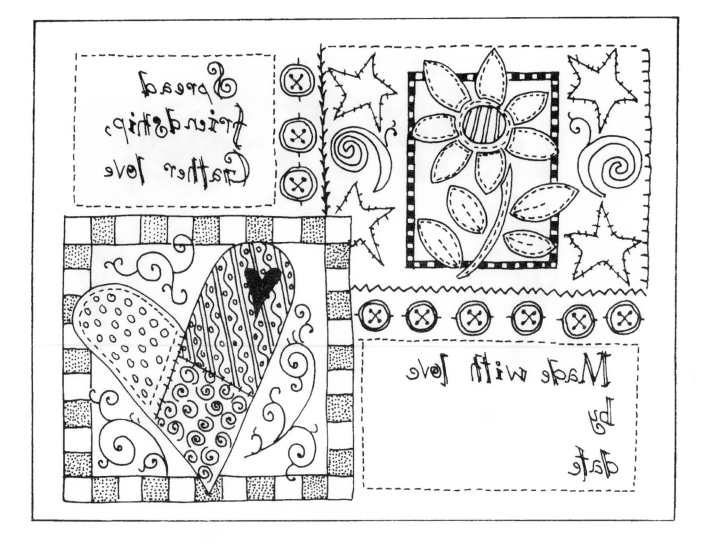

45

Test Pattern

47